Big Trucks

Written by
Jill Atkins

Ransom

A big truck has a cab and a trailer.

The trailer fixes on the back of the cab.

This truck has lots of lights.

She is sitting in the cab of her truck.

4

This truck is a car transporter.

It is loaded with ten cars. Some cars are on the top and some are on the bottom.

Do you think the cars might drop off the truck?

A big ship has come into port. Now the men on the dock will unload the ship.

Some trucks are waiting near the ship.

Containers swing across from the ship on to the backs of the trucks.

This truck is a freezer truck.
It is at the loading dock.

The freezer goods are loaded
into the back of the truck.

Then the truck can start its trip to bring the freezer goods to the shops.

This truck is not so big.

It has a load of rubbish.
The rubbish is in sacks
on the back of the truck.

Truckloads of odd things!

How did that boat get on to the back of that truck?

How come a T-Rex is in the back of this truck?

This smart red truck
has twin trailers.

This truck has twin trailers, too.

It has a long load of tree logs.

This truck is tipping the back up, so the rocks are off-loaded from the back of the truck.

Some trucks are so long!

But some trucks are so **big!**

Is this truck bigger than all the trucks on the planet?